Time to Play

by Ellen Lawrence

Published in 2015 by Ruby Tuesday Books Ltd.

Editor: Mark J. Sachner
Designer: Emma Randall
Production: John Lingham

Photo credits:
Alamy: 4 (bottom), 9 (right), 10, 16, 19, 22; Corbis: 6–7, 17, 22; Cosmographics: 22; FLPA: Cover, 2, 8–9, 13, 20 (left), 22; Sendacow.org. uk: 21 (left), 22; Shutterstock: 4 (top: Tom Gigabite), 5 (top left: Elena Dijour), 5 (bottom left: Martchan), 5 (right: utcon), 11 (Aleksandar Todorovic), 12, 14–15 (utcon), 18, 20 (right), 21 (right: Wasu Watcharadachaphong), 22, 23 (left: utcon), 23 (right: Tom Gigabite).

Library of Congress Control Number: 2014958142

ISBN 978-1-910549-06-3

Printed and published in the United States of America

For further information including rights and permissions requests, please contact our Customer Service Department at 877-337-8577.

The picture on the front cover of this book shows children in Rwanda riding wooden bikes. Turn to page 8 to find out more about how adults and children use wooden bikes in Africa.

Contents

Words shown in **bold** in the text are explained in the glossary.

All the places in this book are shown on the map on page 22.

It's Time to Play!

In Thailand, jumping rope is a popular game. Children make their own long ropes by looping lots of rubber bands together.

In the United States, a playground, a broom handle, and a tennis ball are all that's needed for a game of stickball.

In France, boys and girls hold on tight to this playground carousel.

These boys in Ethiopia are enjoying an outdoor game of foosball.

Taking turns at wheelbarrow rides is great fun for these kids in Vietnam.

A Game of Soccer

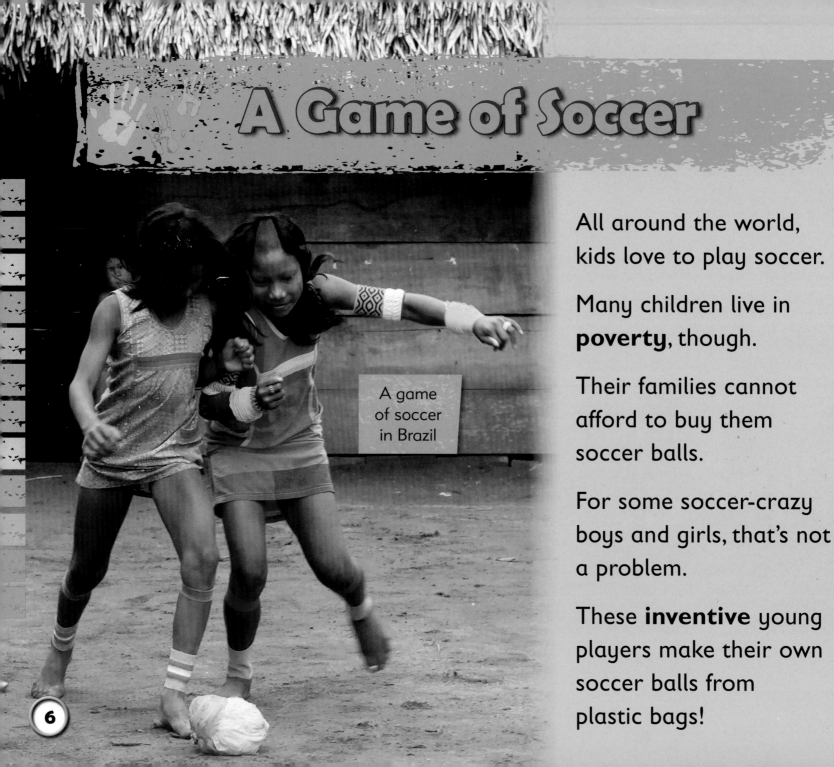

A game of soccer in Brazil

All around the world, kids love to play soccer.

Many children live in **poverty**, though.

Their families cannot afford to buy them soccer balls.

For some soccer-crazy boys and girls, that's not a problem.

These **inventive** young players make their own soccer balls from plastic bags!

These boys in Kenya are making a soccer ball.

One way to make a soccer ball is to pack scrunched-up newspaper inside a plastic bag. Then the first bag is covered with up to 30 more plastic bags. Finally, the ball of bags is held together with rubber bands, string, or strips of old cloth.

Time for kickoff!

Riding a Bike

Riding a bike is a popular pastime for children all over the world.

In many parts of Africa, kids and adults ride bikes made of wood.

These tough, wooden bikes are used for more than just having fun.

They are also used to carry goods such as fruit and vegetables, and firewood.

Wooden bikes don't have pedals. The rider sits or stands on the bike and pushes along the ground with his or her feet—a little like riding a scooter.

Rolling Tires

An old tire might look like a piece of junk.
It can easily become a fun new toy, though.

In many parts of
the world, children
look for old tires in
garbage dumps.

Then they have fun
rolling and chasing
their tires.

You have to be in good shape to run alongside a fast-moving tire. It also takes skill to keep the tire rolling or make it change direction. These boys in India are using sticks to control their tires.

Kids compete to see who can roll their tire the fastest and farthest.

It's Fun to Swing

Up and down. Up and down. All over the world, kids love to play on swings.

You can swing on an old tire.

You can swing in a playground.

These Baka children live in a **rain forest** in Cameroon.

They have made a swing out of liana vines.

A liana vine

Liana vines are plants with long, thin, bendy stems. The vines grow up from the ground and get tangled in trees. Then the vines dangle back down from the tree branches like ropes and are great for swinging!

Let's Play Tug-of-War

Tug-of-war is played in nearly every part of the world. In Vietnam, it has been a **traditional** contest for centuries.

To win a game, one team must pull the other team over a line drawn on the ground.

Tug-of-war teams usually pull on a rope.

Sometimes, however, children have no rope.

Then they just hold onto each other and pull hard!

There's no limit to how many players can join in a game of tug-of-war. Each team might have just two or three players or as many as 10!

In Afghanistan, people love to fly kites and take part in kite fighting.

During a kite fight, **competitors** try to cut the string of their **opponent's** kite.

They do this with the string of their own kite.

The loser's kite then floats off.

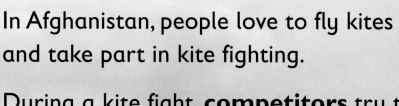

The strings of fighter kites are covered with tiny pieces of crushed glass. This helps the strings cut through the strings of other kites.

A fighter kite

Kids and grown-ups chase
after kites that have been
cut free.

This is called kite running.

The kite runner who catches
a free kite gets to keep it!

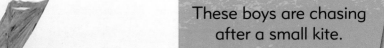
These boys are chasing
after a small kite.

17

Winning Rubber Bands

In many parts of Southeast Asia, children like to play a game with rubber bands.

Each player places a rubber band on the ground.

Then the players begin blowing on their rubber bands.

The object of the game is to blow your rubber band on top of your opponent's.

The winner of a game gets to keep both rubber bands.

Blowing a rubber band to an exact spot isn't easy. Players have to control the direction and speed of the air they blow out. Young players learn their skills by watching older kids and getting lots of practice.

All over the world, children play with their favorite toys. The toys may look very different, but they are all the same in one important way—kids love them!

These boys are sailing their homemade boats in the sea.

This toy bus is made out of wire and other pieces of trash.

This girl loves her doll made from the leaves of a banana plant.

It's a challenge to balance and run on coconut shells.

Where in the World?

Canada
Page 12

France
Page 5

Uganda
Pages 20–21

Afghanistan
Pages 16–17

India
Page 11

Thailand
Pages 4 and 21

North
America

Europe

Asia

Benin
Page 10

Africa

United States
Pages 4 and 12

Vietnam
Pages 5 and 14–15

South
America

Australia

Brazil
Page 6

Sumba, Indonesia
Pages 18–19

Cameroon
Page 13

Rwanda
Pages 8–9

Kenya
Page 7

Madagascar
Page 20

Ethiopia
Page 5

Glossary

competitor (kuhm-PEH-ti-tur)
A person who takes part, or competes, in a game or sport.

inventive (in-VEN-tiv)
Being able to think up unusual ideas, or make new and different things.

opponent (uh-POH-nuhnt)
The person playing against you in a game or sport.

poverty (PAH-vur-tee)
Being very poor without enough money to buy essential things such as food or fuel.

rain forest (RAYN FOR-ist)
A thick forest of tall trees and other plants where lots of rain falls.

traditional (truh-DI-shuh-nuhl)
Something that has been done in a certain way for many years by a group of people. For example, playing a game or taking part in a sport.

Index

B
Baka people 13
bikes 8–9
boats 20
buses (toy) 20

C
coconut shells 21

D
dolls 21

F
foosball 5

H
homemade toys 4, 6–7,
   8–9, 10–11, 20–21

J
jumping rope 4

K
kites 16–17

L
liana vines 13

P
plastic bags 6–7
playgrounds 4–5, 12
poverty 6

R
rain forests 13
rubber bands 4, 7,
   18–19

S
soccer 6–7
soccer balls 6–7
stickball 4
swings 12–13

T
tires 10–11, 12
tug-of-war 14–15

W
wheelbarrow rides 5

Read More

Miller, Amanda. *This Is the Way We Play (Scholastic News Nonfiction Readers)*. New York: Children's Press (2009).

UNICEF. *A Life Like Mine: How Children Live Around the World*. New York: DK Publishing (2002).

Learn More Online

To learn more about play around the world, go to
www.rubytuesdaybooks.com/play